T ☆ H ☆ E
PACIFIC STATES

DON LAWSON

FRANKLIN WATTS
NEW YORK★LONDON★TORONTO★SYDNEY★1984
A FIRST BOOK

Cover photographs courtesy of:
National Park Service, Frank Sloan,
Shostal

Maps courtesy of Vantage Art, Inc.

Photographs courtesy of:
The Bancroft Library: p. 4; California Office of
Tourism: pp. 8, 11; Frank Sloan: p. 9; California Mission
Trails Association: p. 14; California State Library: p. 17; California Historical Society: p. 18; Oregon
Department of Transportation: pp. 24, 28, 33; Portland Visitors and Convention Bureau: p. 26; National
Park Service: p. 39; U.S. Geological Survey: pp. 40,
68; Bureau of Reclamation: p. 43; New York Public
Library: pp. 45, 53; Seattle Visitors and Convention
Bureau: p. 49; Alaska State Division of Tourism: pp.
56, 63; Alyeska Pipeline Service Co.: p. 60; Museum
of the American Indian, Heye Foundation: p. 64;
Library of Congress: p. 67; Hawaii Visitors Bureau:
pp. 76, 79, 84, 87.

Library of Congress Cataloging in Publication Data
Lawson, Don.
The Pacific states.

(A First book)
Includes index.
Summary: Briefly surveys the people, climate,
geography, resources, history, industry, and future of
California, Oregon, Washington, Alaska, and Hawaii.
1. Pacific States—Juvenile literature. 2. Alaska—
Juvenile literature. 3. Hawaii—Juvenile literature.
[1. Pacific States. 2. Alaska. 3. Hawaii] I. Title
F851.L43 1984   979   83-16719
ISBN 0-531-04733-4

CONTENTS

INTRODUCTION

Five states in the United States have one thing in common. At least one of their borders is washed by the warm waters of the Pacific Ocean. For this reason they are often called the Pacific states. These five states are California, Oregon, Washington, Alaska, and Hawaii.

Two of these states, Alaska and Hawaii, have one thing about them that is different. Their borders do not touch any of the other states. Hawaii is separated from all of the other states by the Pacific Ocean. Alaska is separated from Hawaii by the Pacific and from the rest of the continental United States, or "lower forty-eight," by western Canada.

For a long time the great distances that separated Alaska and Hawaii from what was then the continental United States kept Alaska and Hawaii from becoming states. They were called *territories*. Then the day of jet airplane travel arrived, and distances seemed to shrink. In 1959 Alaska and Hawaii became the forty-ninth and fiftieth states to join the Union.

There is a great variety of people as well as climate and geography in the Pacific states. There is also a great variety in the ways the people there live and work. The history of each of the Pacific states also varies widely from the history of the others. But all of it is exciting.

The story of each of the Pacific states is told in the following chapters. We begin with California.

☆ 1 ☆

CALIFORNIA—
THE GOLDEN
STATE

"Gold! Gold!"

This was the cry heard throughout northern California in the year 1848. Soon the cry spread throughout the United States—and the world. The California Gold Rush had begun.

The gold was discovered at a place called Sutter's Mill along the American River in the Sacramento Valley north of San Francisco. A pioneer landowner, Captain John A. Sutter, had hired a carpenter named James W. Marshall to build a sawmill on the Sutter property. It was Marshall who found the first gleaming gold nuggets.

Word of Marshall's discovery spread quickly, and soon thousands of people flooded into the area. Some came overland across the United States in covered wagons called prairie schooners. Others took the long journey by ship around Cape Horn at the tip of South America. Still others made their way by foot across the Isthmus of Panama. They had to struggle through tropical jungles because the Panama Canal had not yet been built. Many died along the way.

The people who came to California seeking gold were called

While building a mill for John Sutter,
James Marshall discovered gold—and so
began the California Gold Rush in 1848.

"Forty-niners" because 1849 was the year when the actual Gold Rush began. Not many people got rich. But enough did so that get-rich-quick newcomers continued to come to the Golden State, as it has since been called.

Actually California did not become a state until 1850. But from the days of the Forty-niners until today the population has continued to grow by leaps and bounds. It is still the fastest growing and most highly populated state in the Union with about twenty-four million people.

SIZE AND CLIMATE

California is the third largest state in area in the United States. Only Alaska and Texas are larger. The total area of the state is almost 159,000 square miles (411,810 sq km), including more than 2,000 square miles (5,180 sq km) of inland lakes and other water surface. California is a long, narrow state, measuring almost 800 miles (1,287 km) down its center and almost 400 miles (643 km) at its greatest width.

There are actually two California climates. The northern part of the state is a land of forests, mountains, and valleys. Here the climate is generally wet and cool. Southern California is generally warm and dry, and there are even deserts and palm trees. Overall, California has a widely varied climate, from very wet to very dry and from temperate to semitropical. Most parts of the state have only two seasons—a rainy season and a dry season. Northern California's rainy season lasts from October to April. Southern California's rainy season lasts from November to March or April.

GEOGRAPHY

California's geography is as varied as its climate. Along the Pacific Ocean there are rocky cliffs and great sandy beaches. In the north

and northwest there are low Coast Ranges covered with redwood forests. There are trees in California's forests estimated to be between three and four thousand years old. Near the eastern border of the state are higher mountains, their granite peaks soaring to great heights. Mount Whitney (14,495 feet or 4,418 m) is the highest mountain in the lower continental United States. Across the southeast part of the state lies the barren Mojave-Colorado Desert. Death Valley in this area is 282 feet (86 m) below sea level, the lowest point in the United States.

One of California's most interesting physical features is what is called the San Andreas Fault. A *fault* in the earth's surface is a break along which the earth's crust sometimes shifts and moves. Such movements cause earthquakes, which are not uncommon in California. The San Andreas Fault runs from the Pacific coast in northern California well into southern California.

The many valleys between the state's numerous mountains provide sheltered and fertile areas for growing crops. One of the biggest of these is the Central or Great Valley which lies between the mountains of the Coast Range and the Sierra Nevada to the east. This huge valley is 400 miles (643 km) long and is one of the most important agriculture areas west of the Rocky Mountains. In it almost every kind of crop is raised. There are also verdant valleys in the northern Cascade Range and irrigated valleys in the desert area of the southeast.

The Central Valley, the irrigated Imperial Valley, and several others have made it possible for California to lead all of the states in farm income.

CALIFORNIA'S CITIES

Although income from agriculture is of great importance to California, most of the state's people live in its numerous large towns,

*Left: California's contrasting terrain includes
the majestic redwood forests in the northwest and
Death Valley near the southeastern Nevada border.
Above: Los Angeles, from the Pasadena Freeway.*

cities, and urban areas. The capital of California is Sacramento. The state's largest cities are Los Angeles, San Diego, San Francisco, San Jose, Long Beach, and Oakland.

CALIFORNIA'S RICH RESOURCES

Few states have the rich natural resources of California. In addition to its favorable climate and fertile soils, an abundant water supply aids in the production of bountiful crops. Even areas that were once barren desert now are irrigated and produce valuable fruits, vegetables, and cereal grains. California leads the nation in fruit and vegetable processing, and its vineyards produce grapes for wines that rival those of France.

Power for homes and industry is provided by hydroelectric plants along the Sacramento and other of the state's rivers. There are also huge deposits of oil and natural gas that provide additional power. Power, of course, is vital to such major California industries as aircraft and automobile manufacturing, shipbuilding, and steel processing.

Important forest resources include fir and pine trees that grow in the mountainous Sierras, Cascades, and southern California's high ranges. In the north there are valuable redwood trees. Sequoias are found along the western slopes of the Sierras.

California's fishing industry rivals that of its sister Pacific state, Alaska. Huge harbors at cities such as San Francisco and San Diego enable California to be a leader in the export and import trade.

Three visitors view rolling California vineyards. Wines made from California grapes are among the best in the world.

Gold is no longer a major source of the state's wealth, but other minerals are. In addition to oil and natural gas, these include cement, sand, gravel, and what was once a little-known product called silicon. Silicon is the material on which miniaturized circuits are etched for use in computers. Near San Francisco an area known as *Silicon Valley* has within recent years developed into the world's most advanced computer technology center.

TOURISM AND THE
MOTION PICTURE INDUSTRY

California's climate and varied scenery have made the state a favorite among tourists from all over the world. Annually up to eight million persons visit the state. In addition to numerous national parks and forests, favorite tourist attractions are the theme park Disneyland at Anaheim, and Hollywood, famed motion picture center of the world and home of the movie stars near Los Angeles.

Beginning in 1908 when *The Count of Monte Cristo* was first filmed there, Hollywood soon became the motion picture capital of the world. Today far fewer pictures are actually filmed there than in Hollywood's heyday, but it is still the world's major source of motion pictures for both theaters and home television.

THE PEOPLE—
PAST AND PRESENT

The first people in California were Indians. These native tribes were a simple, peaceful people who lived on the seeds and roots of the local vegetation. They did, however, clash with the first white settlers who came into the area. The Indians were finally defeated by the whites in the Modoc War of 1873. Remnants of these seed-gathering tribes were placed on reservations, where some of their descendants still live today. Other Indians are scattered throughout the state.

At the time of the Gold Rush there were about fifteen thousand Spanish people living in California. Their society was swept away by the hordes of gold-seeking Forty-niners. Soon California began to be settled by people from every state and from various foreign countries. Early foreign settlers came from Mexico, Canada, Europe, China, and Japan.

California's foreign population remained heavily outnumbered by American white people and a large black minority until the 1970s and 1980s. Then a great wave of foreign immigrants flooded into the state. These people came mainly from Mexico, Central and South America, and Asia. According to the 1981 census, about three-quarters of California's population of 24,196,000 people was still made up of so-called Anglos (whites of non-Latin origin), but Hispanics now make up 19 percent of the state's population and Asians 6 percent. These percentages are expected to grow steadily in the next decade.

Los Angeles has the largest community of Mexicans outside Mexico City, and the largest Korean community outside the Orient. More than a score of foreign languages are spoken in the city's schools. By the mid-1980s Hispanics may become the majority population in Los Angeles.

One of California's future concerns may be racial problems such as those that occurred in the 1960s. In 1965 rioting broke out in the black section of Los Angeles called *Watts*. Before it had ended, many people were killed, others injured, and property damage amounted to more than two hundred million dollars.

HISTORY OF THE GOLDEN STATE

The steadily rising tide of Hispanic people in modern California actually had its beginnings several centuries ago. In 1542 Spanish

The Carmel Mission, established by
Father Junipero Serra in 1770, was the second
Franciscan mission founded in California.

explorer Juan Cabrillo anchored his ship in what is now San Diego harbor and claimed the land for Spain. Somewhat later, English explorer Sir Francis Drake claimed the San Francisco area for England, but Spain's claims were strengthened early in the seventeenth century when Sebastian Vizcano charted the California coast. It was not until the next century, however, that Spain began to colonize the area. They did this to prevent Americans from the east and Russians from Alaska from taking over California.

During the late 1700s and early 1800s Spanish pioneers founded a string of some twenty Franciscan missions northward from San Diego. Numerous towns grew up around these missions, and great cattle ranches were created in the surrounding countryside. During this period governmental control of the area was largely in the hands of Catholic priests and Franciscan monks operating out of Mexico.

But the Americans could not be kept out of California. Yankee sea captains in clipper ships called at the various harbors for trade. Fur traders blazed trails into California from the east. Land-hungry Americans braved the wilderness of deserts and mountains to reach warm, fertile, lush California that already had a reputation as the promised land. Soon it became United States government policy to free California from Mexico and make it part of the United States. The United States, in fact, offered to buy California from Mexico, but the offer was refused.

Mexico had gained its independence from Spain in 1821. California had become a province of Mexico in 1822. The Mexican government had then halted the missionary work of the Franciscan monks in California, but it did not give up any claims to the land. Instead it sent a series of Mexican governors to California.

An American soldier and explorer, John C. Frémont, played an important role in freeing California from Mexico. He led two military exploration parties into the area in 1844 and 1846. When the Mexicans ordered Frémont and his soldiers to leave in 1846, he refused to go and raised the United States flag at a fort he and his men had begun to build near Monterey. Later Frémont and his men withdrew before any fighting began, but soon the United States and Mexico went to war.

Shortly after the war began, a group of American settlers at Sonoma in northern California seized the Mexican headquarters there and raised a homemade flag bearing a star, a grizzly bear, and the inscription *California Republic*. This incident was known as the Bear Flag Revolt. The revolt did not accomplish very much, but soon U.S. soldiers under Frémont, General Stephen Kearny, and others moved into the area to set it free.

In 1848 the United States won the Mexican War, fought partly over the ownership of California, and Mexico surrendered the state in the Treaty of Guadaloupe Hidalgo. California then became a part of the United States. That same year gold was discovered, and soon all of the new California residents began demanding that California become a state. On September 9, 1850, California became the thirty-first state in the Union.

Between the time of the Gold Rush and the United States Civil War, California's population grew from just a few thousand people to almost half a million. After the Civil War ended in 1865, there was a new wave of immigration. This took the form of a "land rush" by people eager to obtain land at low prices.

In 1869 California was linked to the eastern United States by the first transcontinental railroad. Later this railroad became a part of the Southern Pacific, one of the links in a great railroad network that spread from the eastern United States throughout the West. Thousands of Chinese laborers called *coolies* were imported from China and paid low wages to help build these railroads. Many of these Chinese later settled in Los Angeles and San Francisco, where they lived in separate sections of the cities called *Chinatown*.

The Gold Rush swelled California's population.
Here a woman brings lunch to miners working
their claim. The chute, called a long-tom, was
used to sift out gold by a washing process.

San Franciscans survey their ruined city
from Telegraph Hill four days
after the 1906 earthquake.

In 1906 a terrible earthquake and fire struck San Francisco, destroying most of the city and killing 452 people. But the city was soon rebuilt, and its population continued to grow. California's population also expanded greatly all through the first half of the twentieth century.

California's great growth resulted, in part, from the huge increase in irrigated farming, the development of oil and gas wells, mining, and the establishment of the motion picture industry as well as numerous manufacturing industries. The completion of the Panama Canal in 1914 also greatly shortened the distance ships had to travel to reach California from the eastern United States and Europe. This increased trade and further swelled the population.

The Great Depression of the 1930s, when the American economy nearly collapsed and unemployment rose to record levels, brought a new kind of immigrant to California. This was the migrant farm worker who could not find a job elsewhere and headed for California, where it was at least warm. Migrant farm workers flooded into California by the thousands, creating serious employment and welfare problems for the state. These problems were not wholly solved until World War II when California's aircraft and shipbuilding industries, like industry everywhere, expanded enormously to meet the nation's war needs.

After World War II California continued to grow and prosper. In fact, for several decades California maintained a growth rate of almost half a million people a year. This great migration necessitated the development of more businesses and industries, more schools, more retirement facilities for retirees who have flocked into the area to seek the sun, more and better roads and highways, and, in fact, more of everything. But to date California has continued to meet the challenge. To millions of Americans as well as people throughout the world it remains the Golden State.

FUTURE OF
THE GOLDEN STATE

A forewarning for the future in California may have occurred in the spring of 1983 when a severe earthquake struck the little town of Coalinga in the fertile San Joaquin Valley. Fortunately, no one was killed, but some fifty people were injured and several hundred buildings were destroyed, causing thirty million dollars worth of damage.

Coalinga is located more than 20 miles (32 km) from the San Andreas Fault along which scientists predict a major earthquake will occur one day. The Coalinga quake measured 6.5 on the Richter or earthquake scale, but scientists say the San Andreas Fault will eventually cause a quake, or *temblor*, measuring 8 or higher on the Richter scale.

Barring such a major upheaval, the future of California appeared bright in the early 1980s. The face of the state will continue to change with the new waves of immigration, and this may cause further social problems. But the Golden State has a golden reputation for successfully absorbing newcomers, and the absorption of these new immigrants should prove to be no exception.

Economically, California is riding the crest of the wave of the future with such high technology development centers as that in Silicon Valley near San Francisco. Los Angeles, too, was rapidly becoming a "high tech" center as well as a focal point for international trade throughout the Pacific-Asia area. The whole of California, in fact, may well play a key role in future United States-Pacific-Asia social relations and trade.

The eyes of the world will also be on Los Angeles during the summer of 1984, when the International Olympic Games are held there. This will be the second time that Los Angeles has hosted the summer Olympics. The first time was more than half a century ago, in 1932.

The name *California* comes from
a sixteenth century Spanish book,
Las Sergas de Esplandian,
by Garcia Ordonez de Montalvo.

year admitted to the Union: 1850
capital: Sacramento
nickname: the Golden State
motto: Eureka (Greek word for *I have found it.*)
flower: the golden poppy
bird: the California valley quail
song: "I Love You California"
flag: Shows a grizzly bear, symbol of independence.
     There is a lone star and the words
     California Republic. (California was not part
     of the Union when this flag was first used.)

☆2☆

OREGON— THE BEAVER STATE

"Fifty-Four Forty or Fight!"

That was a slogan that helped elect James K. Polk, the eleventh president of the United States, in 1844. The slogan grew out of a dispute between Great Britain and the United States over the vast area then known as Oregon.

In the early 1800s *Oregon* meant all of the land between California and Alaska. Four countries vied for control of this area and its rich fur trade. The countries were Spain, Russia, Great Britain, and the United States. In 1825 Spain and Russia gave up their claims, but the dispute between Great Britain and the young United States continued.

When Polk ran for president against Henry Clay, Polk said that if he were elected, he would settle this dispute. He would do so by having the United States take over the Oregon area up to the northern latitude of 54°40'. He would do so, Polk said, even if it meant war. Thus the slogan, *Fifty-Four Forty or Fight!*

After Polk was elected, the dispute was settled peaceably in a treaty that set the 49° parallel of latitude (except for Vancouver Island) as the official dividing line. The United States took over the area south of this line, and Great Britain took over the area north of it. Today, of course, the state of Washington is immediately north of this line, and the state of Oregon is south of Washington. But it was not until 1859 that Oregon became the thirty-third state to join the Union.

SIZE AND CLIMATE

Oregon is an almost rectangular state, extending 395 miles (635 km) from east to west and 295 miles (475 km) from north to south. Its area covers about 97,000 square miles (251,230 sq km) including almost 800 square miles (2,072 sq km) of inland waters.

The Pacific Ocean has a great influence on Oregon's climate. Warm, wet winds from the Pacific give the western part of the state cool summers and mild winters. This part of the state is, in fact, unusually mild for an area as far north as Oregon.

Eastern Oregon, however, has relatively cold winters and hot summers. This is because eastern and western Oregon are separated by the mountains of the Coast Range and the Cascades. West of the mountains rain and snow are relatively heavy, especially in some areas along the coast where precipitation reaches more than 130 inches (330 cm) a year. After the winds cross the mountains, they become dryer. Eastern Oregon thus lies in what is called a *rain shadow*. It has much less rain and snow, and its climate is also less moderate.

GEOGRAPHY

Oregon's scenic beauty is matched by that of few other states. It has, in fact, been called the Switzerland of North America. Its high mountains, huge forests, and great rivers do indeed make it a scenic wonderland. And its Pacific Ocean coastline, with its rolling sand dunes and craggy cliffs, provides one of the most beautiful marine borders in the world.

—23—

Oregon is divided from north to south by the Cascade Range. Mount Hood (11,245 feet or 3,427 m), which is Oregon's highest peak, is in the Cascades. West of the Cascades are fertile valleys and thick forests. Along the Pacific is the low and rolling Coast Range. In the north the great Columbia River has been harnessed to provide hydroelectric power for homes and factories.

There are many lakes throughout the state. Crater Lake in the Cascades, almost 2,000 feet (609 m) deep, is the deepest lake in the United States.

Almost half the state is covered by forests. Oregon leads all of the states in lumbering, and paper manufacturing is also a major industry. Inland, the Willamette River's huge and fertile valley is a famous fruit-growing area. Crops and livestock are also raised here and elsewhere throughout the state, making agriculture a vital part of Oregon's economy.

The only generally arid region is in the southern part of Oregon. Bordered on the west by the Klamath Mountains, the Great Basin is a semidesert area that extends into California and Nevada.

OREGON'S CITIES

Most of Oregon's largest cities are in the Willamette Valley west of the Cascades. Salem is the state capital. Even though Portland, the state's largest city, lies more than 100 miles (160 km) inland

Beautiful Crater Lake was formed thousands of years ago when Mt. Mazama erupted so violently that it collapsed, leaving a cauldron that eventually filled up with snowmelt and rainwater.

Portland, Oregon's largest city

from the Pacific at the junction of the Willamette and Columbia Rivers, it is a major seaport.

The state's largest cities are Portland, Eugene, Salem, Springfield, Corvallis, Medford, and Gresham.

RESOURCES OF THE BEAVER STATE

Like the other Pacific states, Oregon is rich in resources. Its greatest resource is its vast forests which cover some 30 million square acres of land and produce a quarter of the nation's timber. The main commercial trees are Douglas fir and ponderosa pine. Because its forests are so important to the state's economy, Oregon has long had an outstanding forest conservation program. Timberlands are run on what is called a *sustained yield* system. This means that the planting of new trees equals or exceeds the cutting down of fully grown trees.

Besides forestry the state's leading industries are manufacturing, food processing, agriculture, and tourism. Chief manufactured products are lumber, processed foods, machinery, paper, and transportation equipment. Among the principal agriculture crops are wheat, hay, potatoes, snap beans, cherries, pears, and other fruit. Livestock are raised in the ranges east of the Cascades, and there are large herds of dairy cattle in western Oregon. Sheep and hogs are raised in various areas throughout the state.

Oregon's main harbors are at Portland, Astoria, Newport, and Coos Bay. From these ports are shipped not only the state's farm, dairy, fruit, food, and manufactured products but also its rich harvest of seafood. Among these valuable seafood resources are world-famous Chinook salmon, tuna, Dungeness crab, shrimp, trout, and oysters. Men and women also come from all over the world to fish for Oregon's Chinook salmon and steelhead trout.

Mineral resources include nickel, stone, sand, gravel, and

*Harvesting summer wheat, with
snowcapped Mt. Adams in the background*

bauxite (aluminum ore). Small deposits of gold, silver, copper, and uranium are also found in the state's mountain regions.

OREGON'S PEOPLE—
PAST AND PRESENT

The first white settlers in Oregon encountered numerous Indian tribes. In the north and northwest were the Chinook and Yakima tribes, who lived mainly on the region's bountiful fish. The Nez Percé tribes, in eastern Oregon, were among the last to surrender their lands to the whites. In the south and southeast were the Modoc, Klamath, and Paiute.

Wars against the white settlers greatly reduced the Indian population and finally ended in their defeat. The few thousand who were left were placed on reservations where a handful still live today. Several thousand other Indians are also scattered throughout the state.

Most of the first white settlers were Americans and Canadians. Later Chinese and Japanese laborers were imported from the Orient. Today most of Oregon's population (1981 census: 2,651,000) is American born, but there is also a sizable number of foreign-born Oregonians. Most of the latter originally came from Canada. About 1 percent of the state's population is black.

HISTORY—THE LEWIS
AND CLARK EXPEDITION

Spanish sailors were probably the first explorers to sight what is now Oregon in the sixteenth century. Britain's Sir Francis Drake also touched along the Oregon coast. And Britain's George Vancouver mapped the coast from 1792 to 1794. But it was an American clipper ship captain, Robert Gray, who actually landed on the coast and late in the eighteenth century discovered and named the Columbia River after his own flagship. Gray's discovery, supported by an overland expedition into the area by two famous explorers, Meriwether Lewis and William Clark, resulted in the United States laying claim to the area.

Lewis and Clark were two of the most important explorers in American history. In 1804 President Thomas Jefferson put them in charge of an expedition to explore the vast Louisiana Purchase, which had just been bought from France and added to the United States. Jefferson also wanted the expedition to explore a new land route to the Pacific Ocean. Fur trappers and traders had brought back reports of the great wealth in furs and minerals in the Oregon territory, and it was important for American settlers to have an overland route into the area.

Lewis and Clark and their small party of soldiers, frontiersmen, and Clark's black servant, York, started up the Missouri River from a point near St. Louis in the spring of 1804. More than eighteen long and grueling months later they came in sight of the Pacific Ocean. Along the way they endured every kind of hardship from severe weather to near starvation. Crossing the towering Rocky Mountains was the hardest part of their journey, but here as elsewhere they were greatly helped in making their way by a Shoshone Indian woman named Sacagawea.

Sacagawea was a valuable guide and the wife of Toussaint Charbonneau, a French trapper Lewis and Clark had hired as an interpreter to talk with the various Indians whose lands they would be passing through on the way west. Actually it was Sacagawea who did most of the interpreting. She also acted as a valuable aide and guide on the journey. While the expedition was at Fort Mandan in North Dakota, Sacagawea gave birth to a baby boy. A few days after the baby was born Sacagawea hoisted him up on her back and carried him there for the rest of the journey. Both Lewis and Clark later said the trip would have been impossible without Sacagawea's assistance.

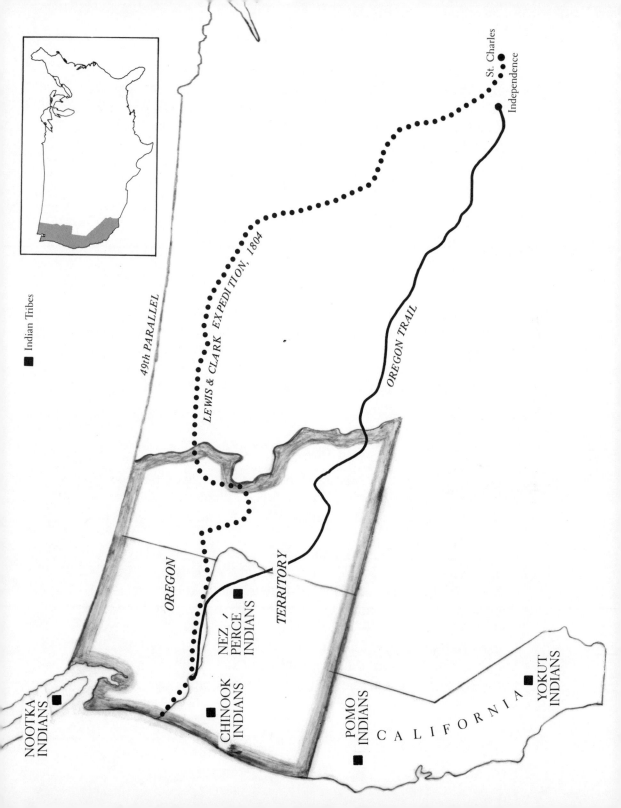

Indian Tribes

St. Charles

Independence

49th PARALLEL

LEWIS & CLARK EXPEDITION, 1804

OREGON TRAIL

OREGON

TERRITORY

NEZ PERCE INDIANS

CALIFORNIA

NOOTKA INDIANS

CHINOOK INDIANS

POMO INDIANS

YOKUT INDIANS

When the Lewis and Clark expedition reached the Pacific, they built a stockade near the mouth of the Columbia River. This stockade was called Fort Clatsop. It was a major basis for the United States claim to Oregon.

THE FATHER OF OREGON

One of the first permanent American fur-trading posts in Oregon was established by John Jacob Astor at Astoria in 1811. A British fur-trading organization, the Hudson's Bay Company, later established a fort and fur-trading post at what is today Vancouver, Washington. In charge of the Hudson's Bay Company's operation was a man named John McLoughlin. McLoughlin eventually became an American citizen and has often been called the Father of Oregon. McLoughlin aided many American settlers who began arriving in the area in the 1840s and 1850s via the Oregon Trail. There were, however, settlers in the Willamette Valley as early as 1834.

THE OREGON TRAIL

Land-hungry, fortune-hunting Americans were eager to get to the fur-rich *Oregon Country* as it was called. Thousands of them got there in wagon trains that traveled the 2,000-mile-long (3,218-km) Oregon Trail.

Most of the Oregon Trail followed the route blazed by Lewis and Clark. Other routes fed into the main trail along the way. The route led from Independence, Missouri, along the Platte River, crossed the Continental Divide to the Snake River, and then led on to the Columbia River. Beyond the Continental Divide some early settlers left the Oregon Trail and made their way into California. Another spur, the Overland Trail, led from the junction of the North Platte and South Platte Rivers to Fort Bridger, Wyom-

Part of a large mural in the
state capitol in Salem, this scene shows a
wagon train resting up before descending
into the Willamette Valley,
on the last miles of the Oregon Trail.

ing. Fort Bridger was named for a famed Indian fighter named Jim Bridger.

The spur into California had been blazed by John C. Frémont and his aide, the mountain man Kit Carson. Carson was a famous trail guide and Indian fighter. He had also made a small fortune trapping beavers in the northern mountains. Along with Frémont and General Stephen Kearny, Carson had helped defeat Mexico in the Mexican War.

Although there was usually little danger from Indian attacks along the main Oregon Trail, expert guides and firm leaders were needed to keep the wagon trains moving through the wilderness country during the summer season. If they delayed into winter, heavy snows made travel impossible. Groups of travelers were organized into militarylike companies, and each was commanded by a captain. Strict discipline was maintained throughout the journey. Even so, hundreds of settlers died along the way.

Settlers who traveled the Oregon Trail in the 1840s and 1850s averaged about 1,000 a year. In 1869 two railroad lines, one from the east and one from the west, met at Promontory Point in Utah. But this first transcontinental railroad did not put an end to the use of the Oregon Trail. Settlers traveled along it up until 1880.

MODERN OREGON

It was the inflow of Americans into the Oregon country that put pressure on the United States to settle the "Oregon Question" with Great Britain and also to make Oregon a state. After the northern boundary of U.S. claims was decided to be the forty-ninth parallel in 1846, the United States Congress created the Oregon territory in 1848. More than a decade later Oregon became the thirty-third state with the boundaries it has today established on February 14, 1859.

During much of this period there was a long series of Indian wars that did not end until 1880. The most tragic of these was perhaps that with the Nez Percé led by Chief Joseph, which began in 1877. Chief Joseph and his people, fighting against being forced onto a reservation, valiantly battled against U.S. troops all the way into Idaho and Montana. Finally Joseph was captured near the Canadian border. All of the Indians in the area were defeated and placed on reservations.

Soon after the first transcontinental railroad was completed, a network of railroads began to spread throughout Oregon and the rest of the United States west coast, connecting several of the Pacific states with the east. This network rapidly led to Oregon's modern development.

FUTURE OF
THE BEAVER STATE

Oregon's economic future depends largely on its huge lumber industry. And the lumber industry depends upon the state of the national economy. During the nationwide economic recession of the late 1970s and early 1980s, lumbering in the Beaver State suffered severely. But as the national economy improved and more new houses were built in the mid-1980s, Oregon forests were again alive with the sound of lumberjacks' saws.

Closely connected with Oregon's forests is the quality of the rest of its natural environment, especially its rivers. Improved water quality is a must if the state is to sustain its steadily growing population. President Ronald Reagan's Council on Environmental Quality (CEQ) reported great improvement in the quality of water in Oregon's Willamette River in 1983. The CEQ predicted further improvement in all of the state's waterways in the future.

The fact that Oregon's population continues to grow is in itself a healthy sign. Unlike several states in the North Central United States whose populations have been declining, Oregon's population has grown by almost half a million people in the past decade and will doubtless continue to grow. Many of these new Oregon immigrants are tourists—tourism is also a major industry in the Beaver State—who come to visit and decide to stay.

Oregon, like many other states, faces future energy problems. It has a champion, however, in native son Donald Hodel. A member of the Oregon Alternate Energy Commission, the Portland-born Hodel was appointed Secretary of the U.S. Department of Energy by President Reagan in 1982. Hodel's many future problems will probably involve overcoming protests of environmental and alternative energy groups who have been critical of his support of nuclear power. Hodel has insisted he favors a balanced energy program, using all sources of power.

The origin of the state's name is not known, but
French Canadians once called the Columbia River
the *Ouragan*, meaning *hurricane* in French.
Major Robert Rogers, a British Army officer,
first reported the use of the name *Oregon*
by Jonathan Carver in 1778.

year admitted to the Union: 1859
capital: Salem
nickname: the Beaver State
motto: the Union
flower: Oregon grape
bird: western meadowlark
song: "Oregon, My Oregon"
flag: On one side is a gold beaver. On the other side
    is the state seal, a shield surrounded by stars.
      The words *State of Oregon* and 1859 also appear.

WASHINGTON– THE EVERGREEN STATE

The only state in the United States to be named for an American president is Washington.

When Washington became a territory of the United States in 1853, there was disagreement over what to call it. The first name suggested was *Columbia* after the Columbia River. But it was thought this name would be confused with the District of Columbia, the nation's capital.

Some people even wanted to call the territory *New York-Alki*. This is what pioneers at Seattle first called their settlement. *Alki* is an Indian word meaning *By and By*, so early Seattle became *New York-Alki*, meaning the tiny settlement would someday be as big and important as New York—"by and by."

President Millard Fillmore and the United States Congress settled the dispute. They agreed that the new territory should be named in honor of the first president, George Washington.

The Washington territory originally included parts of Idaho and Montana. Later a part of Wyoming was also added. The state's present borders were established in 1863, and Washington became the forty-second state in 1889.

SIZE AND CLIMATE

Like Oregon, Washington is roughly rectangular in shape. It extends 354 miles (569 km) from east to west and 237 miles (381 km) from north to south. The state has an area of just over 68,000 miles (109,412 km), some 1,600 square miles (4,144 sq km) of which are inland waters.

Washington's climate is greatly influenced by the Pacific ocean. Warm, wet winds from the Pacific give the western part of the state an even temperature. Here there are relatively cool summers and mild winters. Western Washington also has heavy rainfall, some parts receiving as much as 140 inches (356 cm) of precipitation (rain and melted snow) a year.

The Cascade Range of mountains blocks the Pacific winds from eastern Washington. As a result the eastern part of the state is much drier and has relatively hot summers and cold winters.

GEOGRAPHY

The towering mountains of the Cascade Range divide Washington from north to south. In the Cascades is a Washington landmark, Mount Rainier (14,410 feet or 4,392 m), the highest point in the state. Many of these mountains were once active volcanoes, and in 1980 one of them again became active. This was Mount St. Helens in southwestern Washington. It erupted on May 18 and caused severe damage and much loss of life. Since 1980 there have been smaller eruptions, and scientists say it could erupt again at any time.

Along the Pacific coast are the Olympic Mountains and the Willapa Hills. The latter are part of the Coast Ranges which extend into Oregon and California. In the Olympic Mountains is another famous Washington peak, Mount Olympus.

*Mt. Rainier, in the Cascades,
is the highest point in
the state of Washington.*

The volcanic eruption of Mount St. Helens in *1980*

Puget Sound is a major physical feature of the Evergreen State. West of the Cascade Range, it starts at the Strait of Juan de Fuca—which connects it with the Pacific—and extends southward for about 100 miles (160 km). The Puget Sound trough or lowland runs all the way to the Columbia River, the state's southern border and major river. Most of Washington's cities are located in the Puget Sound trough or lowland area.

East of the Cascades are the Columbia Plateau, the Okanogan Highlands which are a part of the Rocky Mountains, and a small section of the Blue Mountains. In these areas there are numerous fertile river valleys where most of this area's people live. The Yakima Valley is located in south-central Washington and is one of the most fertile farm areas in the nation.

About half of the state is made up of rich forests. These not only give the Evergreen State its nickname but also supply a major portion of the nation's lumber and wood products.

WASHINGTON'S RICH RESOURCES

One of the state's leading timber trees is the Douglas fir, which is grown in the western part of the state. Other valuable trees grown in the Evergreen State are hemlock, spruce, larch, red cedar, and ponderosa pine. The ponderosa pine is grown mainly in eastern Washington. Valuable hardwood trees include alder, aspen, birch, and maple. As in Oregon, there are strict conservation laws that assure the state of continuing growth of new trees to replace or exceed the number of trees that are cut down. Forest fires are among the greatest threats to heavily forested areas, and Washington and Oregon have strict rules and regulations that campers must obey. However, lightning starts many blazes, so forest rangers are on the constant alert for fires in timberland areas following storms.

Most of the land that is not covered with forests is used for crops or as pasture. Wheat is the state's most valuable crop, and apples are second. Washington leads the nation in apple production and ranks second in pear production. Numerous other valuable fruits and cereal grains are also grown throughout the state. Livestock are raised on ranches in eastern Washington, and sheep and dairy cattle are raised in the Puget Sound lowland area.

Among the mineral resources are sand, gravel, cement, stone, and uranium, which are mined in the mountainous areas. The state's most valuable fish are salmon, halibut, flounder, perch, tuna, cod, oysters, and crabs. Washington also has many game birds, animals, and fish that attract hunters and fishermen and -women from all over the world.

Waterpower is one of Washington's most valuable resources. Dams along the length of the Columbia River have produced enormous amounts of hydroelectric power for the state's homes and factories. Grand Coulee Dam on the Columbia is the largest concrete dam in the United States. Columbia River water is also used to irrigate vast tracts of otherwise barren land that has been turned into fertile cropland.

Manufacturing has centered around transportation equipment, mainly the manufacture of aircraft. Major aircraft factories are located at Seattle and Renton. Shipbuilding is also an important industry. Major shipyards are located in port cities in Puget Sound.

WASHINGTON'S CITIES

Seattle is Washington's largest city and a major port. The state capital is Olympia. The largest cities are Seattle, Spokane, Tacoma, Bellevue, Everett, Yakima, Vancouver, Bremerton, and Bellingham.

*The Grand Coulee Dam on the
Columbia River provides waterpower
for much of the state.*

THE PEOPLE OF WASHINGTON
—YESTERDAY AND TODAY

When the white settlers first came to Washington, the major Indians they found were the Chinook tribes, who also occupied what later became the state of Oregon. Most of them lived along the part of the Columbia River that now forms the border between the two states. They were peaceful tribes, living mainly on fish.

Another fish-eating but smaller tribe were the Nootka. They were located along Puget Sound. Washington also shared with Oregon the brave and independent Nez Percé Indians whose fight against being placed on reservations became an American legend.

Washington's Indians, however, like those elsewhere throughout the West, were finally overwhelmed by the white settlers' sheer numbers and were forced onto reservations. Today the largest of these in Washington are at Colville and Yakima. A few Indians live elsewhere throughout the state.

For many years there were just a few thousand whites in what is now Washington. Most of these were British and American fur traders. The opening of the Oregon Trail and the completion of a network of railroads from the East greatly increased the number of Americans in the area. Today only about 5 percent of the state's 4,217,000 residents (according to the 1980 census) are foreign born, most of whom are Canadian. Blacks make up about 3 percent of the population.

HISTORY OF
THE EVERGREEN STATE

Because both Washington and Oregon were originally part of the vast Oregon Country, their early history is much the same. The coast of what is now Washington was visited by Spanish explorer

Indian traders, their horses laden
with furs, arrive at a fur trading post
on the Columbia River.

Bruno Heceta, American clipper ship captain Robert Gray, and British ship captain George Vancouver in the late eighteenth century. Then Meriwether Lewis and William Clark explored much of the region for the United States on an overland expedition early in the nineteenth century. (The Lewis and Clark expedition is described in greater detail in the preceding chapter on Oregon.)

All of this area was rich fur country, so both Great Britain and the United States wanted to own it. These rival claims were supported not only by early explorations but also by fur trading posts. These posts were set up by British Canadians at Spokane in 1810 and by Americans under John Jacob Astor, first at Astoria in today's Oregon, then at Washington's Fort Okanogan in 1811.

In 1836 an American missionary, Marcus Whitman, and his wife, accompanied by Henry Spalding and his wife, founded a mission near Walla Walla, Washington. Mrs. Whitman and Mrs. Spalding were the first white women to cross the American continent. In 1847 the Whitmans were killed by Indians, which led to the brief Cayuse Indian War.

The British-American dispute for this whole area almost led to a war between the two nations. But finally it was decided that the forty-ninth parallel of latitude should divide the British and American territories. Britain, however, kept Vancouver Island. Today the forty-ninth parallel forms Washington's northern border with Canada.

THE PIG WAR

No sooner was this border dispute settled than another territorial disagreement took place over who owned the San Juan Islands just off Washington's northwest coast. Both Britain and the United States claimed the rights to them. The death of a pig caused this dispute to erupt into a minor war.

In 1859 an American living on the main San Juan island killed an English settler's pig. This apparently trivial incident flared into a brief conflict between the United States and Great Britain over which nation's laws governed the area. Britain claimed its local court should decide responsibility in the matter, and the United States insisted its court should rule. The Pig War was finally settled when a court of international arbitration headed by Germany's Kaiser Wilhelm I decided that the San Juan Islands belonged to the United States.

FROM TERRITORY
TO STATE

Soon after the Washington territory was created in 1853 with its capital at Olympia, American settlers in the area began to clamor for statehood. Formal statehood requests were made in 1861, 1867, and 1878. But each time the United States Congress denied the request. Washington, it was claimed, was too remote from the rest of the continental United States and too difficult to get to. But a Northern Pacific railroad link into Washington from the East finally convinced the federal government that Washington should indeed be a part of the Union. Finally, on November 11, 1889, President Benjamin Harrison named Washington as the forty-second state. The territorial capital at Olympia remained the state capital.

Late in the nineteenth century gold was discovered in Alaska and in Canada's Klondike region. These discoveries led to a gold rush that rivaled the one in California during the days of the Forty-niners half a century earlier. The Alaskan Gold Rush is told about in the next chapter on Alaska. Prospectors used Washington and particularly Seattle as an outfitting center and jumping off place on their way to these new gold fields in the far north.

WARTIME EXPANSION

Washington's shipbuilding industry greatly expanded during both World War I and World War II. In World War II the state's aircraft industry also prospered and continued to grow with the production of jet passenger aircraft during the postwar years. Also during World War II an atomic energy center, the Hanford Works, was built in the central part of the state. This project greatly increased the population of an otherwise remote and somewhat desolate area. Plutonium was first produced in the Richland Hanford plant in 1944.

Washington has made great efforts to expand its economy in areas that do not depend so heavily on the defense industry and on wartime needs. This has been done by continuing to develop the Columbia River Basin Irrigation Project to supply water on a vast scale to agricultural lands throughout much of the state. Oil refineries have also been built at Ferndale and elsewhere to furnish fuel to the Pacific Northwest. And, of course, Washington's famous fruit-growing reputation has continued to be enhanced. Mention of the state's name automatically calls up visions of tasty apples and succulent pears.

The Evergreen State's population has continued to grow, not only among visitors but also among people who come to stay. The state's population, in fact, steadily increased during recent years at a rate of more than fifty thousand people annually.

FUTURE OF
THE EVERGREEN STATE

Like that of Oregon, the health of Washington's lumber industry depends upon the national economy. As the latter improved in the early 1980s, so did the Evergreen State's lumber and lumber products industries.

Seattle, Washington's largest city,
is a major industrial center
and vital seaport.

The nationwide recession and severe competition for passengers among the nation's airlines also resulted in cutbacks in the number of new aircraft being purchased. Since Washington produces a major portion of the nation's civilian as well as military aircraft, these cutbacks hurt that portion of the state's economy. This picture gradually began to brighten in the early 1980s.

Increased federal military spending under the Reagan administration, in both conventional and nuclear armaments, promised to be a boon to the Evergreen State's economy. Nevertheless, continuing efforts were being made to diversify the state's manufacturers into nondefense work. These efforts will be greatly aided by Washington's enormous reserves of hydroelectric and nuclear energy. But Washington's nuclear power industry was suffering from problems due to a decreasing demand for electricity in the last several years and to increased costs in constructing nuclear energy plants. Work on several energy plants was halted, but even so the Washington Public Power Supply System faced possible bankruptcy following a default on $2½ billion worth of municipal bonds in the summer of 1983. There was wide speculation over the possibility of the federal government coming to the rescue of the holders of these bonds. Meanwhile, residential electric rates rose by as much as 80 percent.

The nuclear picture was further clouded by the strong anti-nuclear movement which spread throughout the country during the early 1980s. In Washington it focused on the U.S. Navy's Trident submarine base at Bangor. There, in the spring of 1983, a group of anti-nuclear protesters were arrested and brought to trial for trying to stop a train carrying 100 nuclear warheads for the nuclear-powered, nuclear-armed Trident submarines at the base. The resulting trial gained national attention when the Roman Catholic Archbishop of Seattle, Raymond Hunthausen, testified that "it is all right to break the law to protest nuclear arms because of their unprecedented threat to humanity." Washingtonians expressed a hope that such nonviolent protests would not grow and erupt into violence as they had elsewhere in the United States.

Washington is named in honor of George Washington, the first president of the United States.

year admitted to Union: 1889
capital: Olympia
nickname: the Evergreen State
motto: *Alki* (Chinook Indian word meaning *By and By*)
flower: coast rhododendron
bird: willow goldfinch
song: "Washington, My Home"
flag: In the center is the state seal, a portrait of
George Washington, on a field of dark green.

☆4☆

ALASKA– THE FRONTIER STATE

"Seward's Folly" and "Seward's Icebox."

These were the scornful words many Americans used to describe Alaska when it was bought by the United States from Russia in 1867. The price was $7,200,000, or about 2½ cents an acre. In time the purchase proved to be one of the best bargains any country ever made.

Russia, which is only fifty-one miles (82 km) from the Alaskan mainland, had controlled the Alaskan region since early in the eighteenth century. It was mainly interested in getting the rich harvest of animal furs from the area. But as more and more fur-bearing animals were killed, the fur trade began to die out. Soon Russia lost interest in Alaska and offered to sell it.

Great Britain, whose fur traders and trappers were also active in Alaska, was not interested in buying it. But the United States was. William H. Seward was then U.S. Secretary of State. His offer of slightly more than seven million dollars was agreed to by Russia. The U.S. Congress approved the purchase, and on October 18, 1867, the American flag was first raised at Sitka.

Seward's Folly in time proved to be a stroke of great statesmanship. Not only has Alaska proved to be rich in fish, minerals,

This painting shows the signing of the
Alaska purchase agreement in *1867*.
Seward is seated at left and Russian Minister
Baron de Stoeckel is standing in front of the globe.

and timber as well as furs, but its strategic location in time of war has also been enormously valuable to the United States and its neighbor Canada. The oil and natural gas from just one area of Alaska, that at Prudhoe Bay on the Arctic coast, has repaid the region's original purchase price many times over. Alaskan oil has been made available to the rest of the United States and the world via a huge Trans-Alaska pipeline, which was completed in 1977.

SIZE, LOCATION, AND CLIMATE

Almost everything about Alaska is big. Not only is it the largest state in the United States, but it is also more than twice the size of the next largest state, Texas. Its area of more than 586,000 square miles (1,517,740 sq km) including more than 20,000 square miles (51,800 sq km) of inland water, makes it almost one-fifth the size of the rest of the United States. Alaska also has the highest point on the North American continent, which is Mount McKinley (20,320 feet or 6,193 m). Its coastline of 6,640 miles (10,624 km) is longer than the coastline of all of the other forty-nine states combined.

Alaska occupies the northwest corner of North America. It is a huge, dipper-shaped peninsula from which there are two long arms or extensions. One of these arms extends into the Pacific Ocean and the Bering Sea. The other arm extends along Canada's Yukon territory. All of Alaska's mainland on the east is bordered by Canada. On the north the state is bordered by the Arctic Ocean. On the west are the Bering Sea and Bering Strait, through which runs the International Date Line.

Alaska has a wide variety of climate, ranging from mild and wet to dry and extremely cold. Southern Alaska has relatively mild temperatures, and along the southeast coast there is heavy rainfall. Rainfall is also heavy in the Aleutian Island chain, which is one of the arms extending from the mainland. The Aleutians are cool in summer and cold in winter. The other arm that extends along the

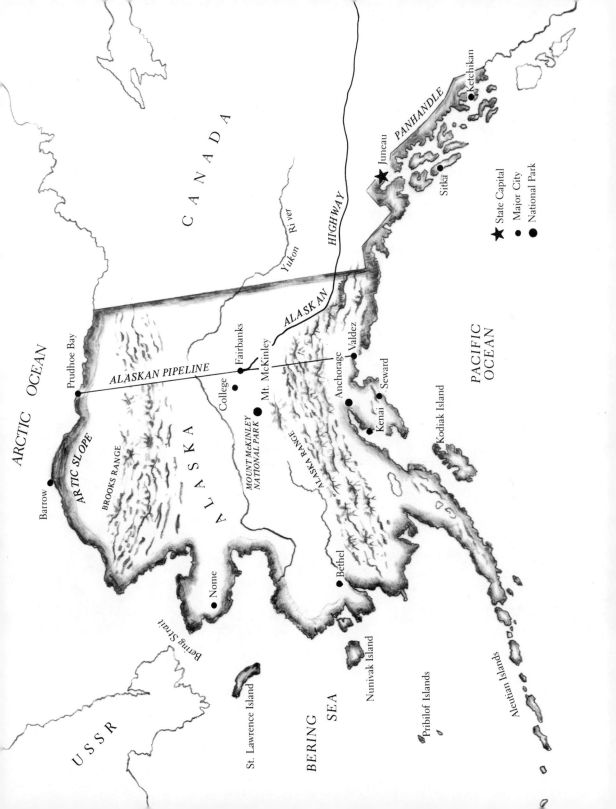

This sweeping valley against a mountain
backdrop is characteristic of interior Alaska.

coast of Canada is also extremely wet. Called the *Panhandle*, this region is an area of great scenic beauty.

The interior of the mainland has moderate amounts of rainfall and temperatures roughly similar to those in the midwest United States. Highs and lows are more extreme, however, with severe sub zero days in winter and hot, ninety degrees–plus days in summer. This is mainly due to the fact that much of the state lies within or near the Arctic Circle, so winter nights and summer days are longer than elsewhere in the United States. Within the Arctic northern region, cold is severe, causing the formation of huge ice packs or fields. In parts of the Arctic, however, temperatures are relatively mild for the brief period from midsummer to early autumn.

ALASKA'S GEOGRAPHY

Alaska has three main geographic regions, southern, the interior, and northern. Southern Alaska is a mountainous area roughly 100 miles (160 km) wide. Here there are numerous high mountains, including Mount McKinley, as well as huge glaciers. The mountains here are part of the Coastal Range which extends along most of western North America. At one time many of these mountains were active volcanoes. Further west in the Aleutian Islands the mountains are much lower and still occasionally display volcanic activity. Mountains in the southeastern Panhandle range up to 10,000 feet (3,048 m), and there are numerous glaciers.

Interior Alaska is an area of broad valleys and hills. It is bordered on the south by the Alaska Range of mountains and on the north by the Brooks Range. This valley area is divided by the lengthy Yukon River flowing out of Canada and into the Bering Sea. Much of interior Alaska is made up of forests, lakes, and swamplands.

In the northern or Arctic region of the state the summer sun remains above the horizon for almost three straight months. When it goes down, however, and the long Arctic night sets in, with temperatures averaging eleven degrees below zero, there is little human activity. Much of this region is a barren, windswept slope covered by permanently frozen ground called *permafrost*. This permafrost is at least 1,000 feet (305 m) thick, and only its surface thaws during the short summer. No trees can grow on this surface—called *tundra*—but there are many beautiful summer wild flowers.

BLACK GOLD AND OTHER RICH RESOURCES

Because much of Alaska remains unexplored, many of its resources remain untapped. This is why it is often called the Frontier State. As such it is also perhaps America's last frontier. Those resources that have been tapped make it one of the richest storehouses of wealth in the world.

At one time the discovery of gold in Alaska and neighboring Canada promised to make this region a continuing source of riches. But as the gold began to run out, this dream faded. But soon it was replaced by a new and even greater one. This grew out of the discovery of oil or *black gold* off Alaska's northern shore.

In 1968 a huge petroleum and natural gas reservoir was discovered at Prudhoe Bay along the Arctic Coast. This reservoir, it was estimated, contained some ten billion barrels of oil and perhaps a third of a trillion cubic feet of natural gas. This made it twice as big as any other oil reserve in North America. At the time of the Prudhoe Bay discovery the United States, along with the rest of the world, was just beginning to experience an oil shortage due to increasing energy needs. Later a number of the major oil-producing countries made the situation worse by temporarily cutting off all of their oil supplies in order to raise the price of the oil they sold. This made it essential to find some way to get Alaskan oil to a port that could be reached by oil tankers. The Arctic Ocean, of course, was ice-locked most of the year.

Finally, the United States decided to finance the building of an oil pipeline from Prudhoe Bay southward across the entire width of the state to the port of Valdez on the Gulf of Alaska and the Pacific Ocean. This huge 800-mile (1,287-km) pipeline was completed in 1977 at a cost of almost eight billion dollars. Oil began to flow through it on June twentieth of that year and since then, with only brief delays due to mechanical problems, black gold has continued to flow steadily from Alaska to an oil-hungry world.

During the 1980s a worldwide recession cut back on the general need for oil as an energy source, but this could only be a temporary situation. Once world economy returned to normal, oil would again be in great demand, and its Alaskan source would undoubtedly prove to be a black-gold mine more valuable than any regular gold mine of the Gold Rush era. Also during the 1980s the United States began to give serious consideration to building a natural gas pipeline to make available the rich reserves of this product that were simply going to waste in the Arctic wasteland.

Alaska also remains rich in other mineral reserves that have not been fully explored or used due to transportation difficulties. These include gold, silver, nickel, tin, lead, zinc, and copper.

FISH, FURS, AND TIMBER

Alaska's fish resources are also important to the state's economy. Most important are salmon, various kinds of shellfish, halibut, and herring. Overfishing has endangered the state's fisheries, but rigid conservation laws have somewhat lessened this danger. Salmon, however, continue to be in short supply in relation to world demands.

*The 800-mile Alaska Pipeline transports
oil from Prudhoe Bay on the Arctic Ocean
to the Pacific port of Valdez.*

The fur industry has also been strictly regulated to prevent the extinction of certain fur-bearing animals. Fur seals in the off-shore Pribilof Islands, for example, are protected by the federal government, and the sale of their skins is handled by the United States with most of the profit going to Alaska.

Other of the state's valuable fur-bearing animals include beaver, marten, lynx, land otter, and muskrat. Mink and fox for furs are mainly raised on farms.

Like Washington and Oregon, Alaska is an important source of lumber and lumber products. Here again, however, transportation problems prevent much of the timberland from being worked because the felled trees cannot be gotten to market economically. Vast areas of spruce, birch, aspen, larch and other trees await the solving of these transportation problems. In the Panhandle, however, Western hemlock, spruce, and cedar are more readily available. In national forests in southern and southeastern Alaska logging is government-regulated and conservation methods similar to those in Washington and Oregon are in effect.

AGRICULTURE AND TOURISM

Not much of Alaska lends itself to farming. Consequently, the state has to import up to 90 percent of its food. Garden vegetables are grown in areas where the growing season is long enough. The best farming regions are in the Matanuska Valley near Anchorage, the Tanana River Valley near Fairbanks, and in the Panhandle.

Tourism is a major Alaskan industry due to the largely untouched scenic beauty of this vast state. Tourists come by air, sea, and even by automobile. Alaska was made available to motoring tourists with the building of the lengthy Alaskan Highway, which is the only land link between Alaska and the rest of the continental United States. Most of this more than 1,500-mile (2,413-km) highway runs through Canada. Originally called the

Alcan Highway, it was built during World War II for defense transportation purposes. It begins in British Columbia and runs up to Fairbanks. Canada owns and maintains the Canadian section of this spectacular highway.

ALASKA'S MAJOR CITIES

Due to the relatively small size of Alaska's overall population, its cities are comparatively small even though that is where most Alaskans live. Juneau is the capital. The state's largest cities are Anchorage, Fairbanks, Juneau, Sitka, Ketchikan, Kodiak, and Bethel.

PEOPLE OF THE FRONTIER
STATE—PAST AND PRESENT

About the only thing that is not big about Alaska is its population. According to the 1980 census there were 412,000 people in the state, giving it the lowest population in the nation. Since then, however, it has grown at a rapid rate.

A relatively large part of the population is made up of native-born Eskimo, Indians, and the so-called Aleuts. These people's ancestors were in Alaska when the first white settlers arrived there.

Eskimo are the most numerous of the nonwhite Alaskans. Indians rank second, and the Aleuts third. The Aleuts are closely related to the Eskimo.

Among the white population many are foreign born. These include people from Canada, Germany, Norway, Sweden, Asia, Great Britain, and the Soviet Union. Americans who themselves or whose ancestors came from the lower continental United States make up the major portion of the state's population.

Juneau, the state capital

An Eskimo family in front of their igloo
made of skins, near Nome around *1910*

ALASKA'S
COLORFUL HISTORY

Vitus Bering, a Danish Explorer hired by Russia, was the first European to land in Alaska in 1741. Bering Strait is named after him. Later in the eighteenth century, Spanish, British, and French explorers searched the area for the legendary Northwest Passage, a sea route between the Atlantic and Pacific Oceans. Britain's Captain James Cook further explored the area in 1778, but there was no Northwest Passage to be found.

By this time, however, the Russians had begun to be interested in Alaska as a source of sea otter furs. The first white settlement on Alaska was set up by Russia's Gregor Shelikoff on Kodiak Island in 1784. This was a fur-trading post.

At the beginning of the nineteenth century the Russians established a fur-trading company on the Alaskan mainland. For the next three quarters of a century this company led by Alexander Baranof governed Alaska.

Baranof was a harsh if efficient ruler. He supplied Russia with an abundance of furs, but to do so he made slaves out of some of the native Aleuts, killed off uncooperative Indians, and made enemies of the Eskimo. Baranof's headquarters were at Sitka, which the Russians called New Archangel. Russian influence on the architecture of Sitka, especially in its churches, can still be seen today.

As the fur trade began to die out—mainly because of the mass slaughter of fur-bearing animals, especially the sea otter—the Russians decided to sell Alaska to the United States. For a long time after its purchase by the United States in 1867, Alaska had no local civil government.

In 1884 it was made a district and governed by the laws of Oregon. The U.S. federal government remained in overall charge of the area.

THE GOLD RUSH

The discovery of gold in Canada's neighboring Klondike region in 1896 ended the American public's lack of interest in Alaska. Thousands of prospectors streamed out of ports of the United States west coast to Alaska and through southeastern Alaska to the Klondike. Within a few months Alaska's population had grown by more than thirty thousand people.

The Klondike gold craze had scarcely died down before gold was also discovered at Nome, Alaska, on the Seward Peninsula in 1899, and a new gold rush began. In 1902 more gold strikes were made near Fairbanks, Alaska, and additional armies of prospectors poured into the region.

When the gold rush ended, interest in Alaska died somewhat. But other valuable minerals had also been discovered there, especially copper, and soon copper-smelting operations had been set up by American companies. Alaska's abundant salmon also led to the establishment of fish canneries along the coast.

FROM TERRITORY TO STATE

It was not until 1912, however, that the United States took firm steps to recognize Alaska as a real part of the nation. In that year President William Howard Taft signed a bill incorporating Alaska as a territory. But Alaska remained pretty much out of the mainstream of American life until the beginning of World War II.

In 1942 American territory was actually invaded by the enemy when the Japanese military forces seized the Aleutian islands of Kiska and Attu. The United States rushed forces to the area and recaptured the islands the following year. But the Japanese threat remained, and the United States, aided by Canada, began to construct the Alcan Highway to enable military forces and supplies to be transported from the United States across Canada to Alaska.

Miners enroute to the Klondike goldfields scale
Jacob's Ladder, as this mountain passage was called.

When World War II ended, the Alaskan Highway was expanded and improved, and much additional military construction was continued in Alaska itself. Soon the state became a bastion of defense, not only for the United States but also for Canada and the rest of North America. Today the anchor of the defense line is at Anchorage where Elmendorf Air Force Base, one of the world's largest air fields, is located. Radar and missile-detection sites have also been strung across Alaska's Arctic wastes to warn of possible attack by Russia.

As Alaska's population grew and its importance to the rest of the nation was recognized, Alaskans and other Americans began to insist that Alaska be made the forty-ninth state. Finally, on June 30, 1958, the United States Congress approved an Alaskan statehood bill. The statehood proclamation was signed by President Dwight D. Eisenhower on January 3, 1959, making Alaska the first new state to be added to the Union since 1912 when both New Mexico and Arizona became states. Alaska too was to have a "twin" entry into the Union. This was Hawaii which also became a state in 1959.

Alaskans had barely begun to enjoy the satisfaction of statehood when southern Alaska was devastated by the most severe earthquake ever to strike North America. It occurred on March 27, 1964, killing more than 100 people and causing damage estimated at more than five hundred million dollars. Anchorage was most severely damaged, but Kodiak, Seward, and Valdez also suffered severely. U.S. federal aid as well as massive aid from private relief organizations and individuals in the "lower forty-eight" states was rushed to people in their stricken sister state. Almost immedi-

The 1964 earthquake left Anchorage and much of southern Alaska devastated.

ately the new United States citizens of Alaska began to rebuild their state, and today the earthquake's scars have all but vanished.

ALASKA TODAY

Since becoming a state Alaska has prospered as have few other states in the United States. Much of this prosperity has come from the huge oil discoveries on its Arctic coast and the building of the oil pipeline. But most Alaskans feel their state has so much untapped wealth besides oil that their prosperity has barely begun. Most outsiders feel this way too, and the state's population has continued to swell with newcomers hoping to share in the prosperity that is bound to follow the conquering of America's last frontier.

FUTURE OF
THE FRONTIER STATE

Alaska's vast size and equally vast untapped resources may present the Frontier State with a special set of problems in the future. Some of these problems have already begun to surface.

When Alaska became a state it already had more square miles set aside as national parks, forests, and game reserves than all of the other forty-nine state combined. But as James Watt, Secretary of the Interior under President Ronald Reagan, pointed out, 99 percent of Alaska was still undeveloped. It was in the interests of the rest of the United States, Watt insisted, for private industry to exploit at least some of this mineral, timber, and other wealth. Alaskans, for the most part, disagreed. This debate will undoubtedly continue.

At the peak of the boom in oil prices, Alaska made so much money from royalties on state-owned oil leases that it repealed its personal income tax. It also embarked on a huge spending program for hydroelectric power projects and the 100 percent funding of public education.

But as the worldwide oil glut continued into the mid-1980s and oil prices dropped drastically, Governor William Sheffield and other state officials began to consider reinstating the personal income tax. Governor Sheffield also urged scaling back such ambitious projects as developing farming in Alaska's interior.

The governor's most controversial proposal, however, was to cancel Alaska's unique petroleum "dividend" program. In 1982 more than 400,000 Alaska residents each received a one thousand dollar dividend check. Sheffield wanted to use the several hundred million dollars earmarked for the petroleum dividend to help finance the state's operating and capital construction costs.

But Alaskans liked the oil dividends, and the threat to cancel them met with much opposition. A former governor, Jay Hammond, insisted that the so-called Permanent Fund Dividend Program, which is financed with earnings from Alaska's $4.2 billion oil revenue savings account, is the only way that all Alaskans can get their fair share of the state's oil riches. This controversy will almost certainly continue in the future.

The name Alaska comes from a similar-sounding
Aleut word meaning *great land* or *mainland*.

year admitted to Union: 1959
capital: Juneau
nicknames: the Last Frontier, the Great Land
motto: North to the Future
flower: forget-me-not
bird: willow ptarmigan
song: "Alaska's Flag"

flag: was designed by a thirteen-year-old boy named Benny Benson in a contest sponsored by the American Legion in 1926. Adopted in 1927, the flag shows the heavenly constellation of seven stars and the North Star, which is known as the Big Dipper. The gold stars are shown against a blue background. In describing his design young Benson said, "The blue field is for the Alaska sky, and the forget-me-not, Alaska's state flower. The North Star is for the future State of Alaska, the most northerly of the Union. [Alaska was not then a state.] The Dipper is for the Great Bear, symbolizing strength."

☆5☆

HAWAII–
THE ALOHA
STATE

The only state in the United States that was once an independent kingdom is Hawaii.

Many other things about Hawaii make it different too. It is the only state that is not a part of the North American mainland. It is the only state made up entirely of islands. It is also the fiftieth and most recent state to join the Union.

Both Alaska and Hawaii gained statehood in 1959. But unlike Alaska, a part of which lies within the Arctic Circle, Hawaii is in the tropics. This gives it the mildest, most even temperatures of all the fifty states. In many ways Hawaii is a tropical island paradise.

Although Hawaii was long a kingdom, it was not always ruled by kings. In fact its last monarch was a queen. Each of its several kings was named Kamehameha. Late in the nineteenth century Queen Liliuokalani became the ruler. She was deposed, and a republic was established in 1894. Several years later the United States took over the islands. But it was not until after the middle of the twentieth century that Hawaii became a state.

SIZE, LOCATION, AND CLIMATE
OF THE ALOHA STATE

Hawaii is a 1,600-mile (2,560-km) chain of more than one hundred islands in the central North Pacific Ocean. Not all of these islands are inhabited. In fact the people of Hawaii live on only seven of the main islands at the southeastern end of the chain. These islands in order of size are Hawaii, Maui, Oahu, Kauai, Molokai, Lanai, Niihau, and Kahoolawe. More than three-quarters of the state's people live on Oahu; Kahoolawe is uninhabited.

Hawaii's overall size of about 6,500 square miles (16,835 sq km) makes it one of the smallest states in land area in the Union. Although it lies more than 2,000 nautical miles from the United States mainland, its strategic location makes it a key military outpost. The Japanese attack on the United States naval base at Pearl Harbor, Hawaii, on December 7, 1941, brought the United States into World War II.

Hawaii's climate is world famous. Although it is in the tropics, cool winds off the Pacific Ocean keep temperatures mild. There are seldom any temperature changes, with averages about 75°F throughout the year. Rainfall, however, varies more widely and is influenced by the northeast tradewinds and the mountains. West of Hawaii's mountains rainfall is relatively light, averaging in some areas only 9 inches (23 cm) a year. East of the mountains rainfall is plentiful. Mount Waialeale on Kauai Island is the wettest place in the world, receiving some 486 inches (1,234 cm) of rain annually. Although Hawaii is in the tropics, it also has some snow. But only on the tops of the highest peaks.

GEOGRAPHY

The Hawaiian islands that are inhabited are the tops of submerged volcanoes. Some of these volcanoes are still active. These include Mauna Loa and its sister peak on Hawaii Island, Kilauea. Mauna

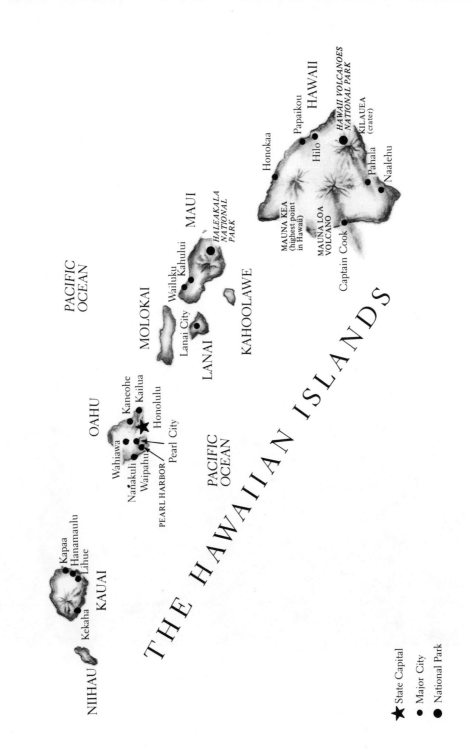

THE HAWAIIAN ISLANDS

PACIFIC OCEAN

PACIFIC OCEAN

HAWAII

Honokaa
Papaikou
Hilo
HAWAII VOLCANOES NATIONAL PARK
KILAUEA (crater)
Pahala
Naalehu
MAUNA KEA (highest point in Hawaii)
MAUNA LOA VOLCANO
Captain Cook

MAUI
Kahului
Wailuku
HALEAKALA NATIONAL PARK

MOLOKAI

Lanai City
LANAI

KAHOOLAWE

OAHU
Kaneohe
Kailua
Honolulu
Wahiawa
Nanakuli
Waipahu
Pearl City
PEARL HARBOR

Kapaa
Hanamaulu
Lihue
Kekaha
KAUAI

NIIHAU

★ State Capital
● Major City
● National Park

Mauna Kea, on Hawaii Island

Loa erupts on an average of every four and a half years and Kilauea every two and a half years. Serious eruptions ocurred from Mount Kilauea as recently as 1983. Mauna Loa (13,680 feet or 4,170 m) and Mauna Kea (13,796 feet or 4,205 m) are the state's highest points.

Throughout the inhabited islands there are numerous mountains and rich, green valleys. Lowlands are found mainly on Molokai Island and Niihau Island.

Most of the smaller, uninhabited Hawaiian islands are low-lying coral reefs partially covered by sand. The surrounding waters abound in fish, but the lack of soil on the islands themselves makes it impossible to grow crops. The soil on the main islands is rich in lava or volcanic ash, so crops such as pineapples and sugar cane can be grown on them.

The geography and climate make plant life abundant. In fact there are some eighteen hundred species of plants in Hawaii. Birds are plentiful throughout all of the islands which once formed one of the biggest birdlife colonies in the world. At one time these birds were killed for their feathers to decorate women's hats, but after as many as three hundred thousand of them were killed in one year, the United States created the Hawaiian Islands Bird Sanctuary in 1909. Bird life, however, has steadily declined but is still abundant. Some of the local seabirds can be found nowhere else in the world.

RICH RESOURCES OF
THE ALOHA STATE

Hawaii's richest resource is its climate. This helps make tourism the fiftieth state's biggest industry. Some five and a half million tourists visit Hawaii annually. Its warm, friendly climate is matched by its warm, friendly people, and the many ancient customs that survive are also valuable tourist attractions.

Visitors are welcomed with a friendly *aloha*, which means simply *greetings* in the Hawaiian language. They may also be presented with a garland or wreath of tropical flowers called a *lei*. Later they may attend a feast called a *luau*, at which a whole roast pig may serve as the main meal accompanied by another traditional dish called *poi*.

At an evening entertainment visitors may see Hawaiian dancers perform a *hula*. Interestingly, this dance was once a sacred performance for the goddess Laka. Day after day the sun shines down, and the cool trade winds blow, while the warm waters of the Pacific wash across Hawaii's golden sand beaches, making visitors want never to leave this charmed land.

Although only about 10 percent of Hawaii's land is available for crops, its soil is nevertheless one of the state's most valuable resources. As much as twelve tons of sugar per acre of sugar cane is yielded from the rich lava-ash soil. Because of the climate, of course, crops can be grown throughout the year, so sugar and pineapple plantations never shut down.

Pineapples are perhaps Hawaii's most widely known crop. Half of the pineapples grown in the world are grown in Hawaii. James D. Dole first canned pineapple successfully in 1903. But the pineapple crop ranks second to sugar in economic importance. To take advantage of the twelve-month growing season, pineapples are planted and harvested in rotation each month of the year. The biggest harvest season, however, is during the summer. Papayas are a relatively recent major export from Hawaii.

Hawaii's two major crops:
sugar cane in bloom (top) and
harvesting pineapples (bottom)

Cattle ranching, dairy farming, and truck gardening are three other important sources of economic income for the state. Most beef, milk, and garden produce are sold locally. Some coffee and a large amount of macadamia nuts are exported. Commercial fishing adds several billion dollars a year to Hawaii's economy. Food processing and the manufacture of construction materials—wood products, cement, and concrete—are Hawaii's main industries. They are located in several of the major cities.

HAWAII'S CITIES

Honolulu, on Oahu Island, the state's largest city, is also the capital. The next largest city is Hilo. It is located on Hawaii Island.

HAWAII'S PEOPLE—
PAST AND PRESENT

Hawaii is truly a melting pot of a wide variety of races. In fact as many as sixty-four racial combinations can be found in the Aloha State. During a time when there is still much racial trouble in the world, Hawaii can serve as a shining example of how different races can get along together harmoniously in a civilized society.

The Hawaiians have a saying: *Above all nations is humanity*. As proof of this the early Hawaiians, the first of whom were Polynesians, welcomed to their shores not only white Americans and Europeans but also Chinese, Japanese, Filipinos, Koreans, Puerto Ricans, and other nonwhite immigrants. Late in the nineteenth century and early in the twentieth century almost half a million laborers were imported from a wide variety of places such as Russia, New Guinea, Italy, and Mongolia to work in the sugar cane and pineapple fields.

Interracial harmony was not achieved automatically. White people not infrequently clashed with Orientals, especially the Japanese, and there were occasional outbursts of friction among the various other races. Gradually, however, good sense prevailed, and today there are few if any racial problems.

Hawaii differs from all of the other states in that only about two of every five of its citizens are white. Most Hawaiians are of Oriental descent. All, however, are Americans.

According to the 1980 census, Hawaii had a population of 965,000. Since then it has probably swollen to more than a million.

JAPANESE-HAWAIIANS
IN WORLD WAR II

The Japanese population of Hawaii proved its loyalty to the Hawaiian Islands and the United States during World War II. Immediately after Japan attacked Pearl Harbor literally thousands of so-called A.J.A's (Americans of Japanese Ancestry) volunteered to fight for Hawaii and the United States. Many A.J.A.'s were inducted into the U.S. Army and sent to fight with the infantry in Europe. Their regimental combat team became the most decorated unit in American military history.

A story about these heroic A.J.A.'s reached the Hawaiian Islands during World War II that is still told there with pride today. When several A.J.A.'s captured a German soldier and brought him back to American headquarters to be questioned by a Japanese captain, the German prisoner said, "But I thought you Japanese were on our side." "You shouldn't believe all that German propaganda," the captain replied.

HISTORY OF THE ALOHA STATE

The first European to sight the Hawaiian Islands was British sea captain James Cook on January 18, 1778. At that time the islands were occupied by primitive Polynesians who had probably sailed there from faraway Tahiti hundreds of years before.

Cook and his men were warmly greeted by the Polynesian-Hawaiians. One of the reasons for their warm greeting was that they thought Cook was one of their ancient gods, Lono, who had returned to earth. Cook gave the islanders a few simple gifts including some nails, which were highly prized because they could be made into fishhooks. In return the Hawaiians loaded Cook's two ships, the *Resolution* and *Discovery*, with fresh pork and sweet potatoes.

Cook remained for only a few weeks and then sailed away to continue his exploration of the Pacific. He did give the islands a name, however. He called them the Sandwich Islands in honor of Britain's Earl of Sandwich, who had paid for the Cook expedition.

About a year later Cook and his men returned to the islands. This time he was again greeted as the god Lono, and he and his men were entertained at feasts and celebrations. But several islanders stole some tools and a boat from one of Cook's ships. They planned to burn the boat to obtain more of the highly prized nails.

Cook demanded that the thieves return these articles. When this was not done, Cook and several of his crew members threatened to take several islanders hostage and hold them until his demands were met. In a skirmish on the beach, Cook was stabbed and clubbed to death. His men managed to recover their captain's body, which they buried with Royal Navy honors in Kealakehua Bay on Hawaii's west coast. The expedition then returned to England to report the discovery of the Sandwich Islands and Cook's tragic death. Several years were to pass before Europeans returned to the islands.

Among the few things left behind in Hawaii by the Cook expedition were several goats. These goats were allowed by the islanders to run wild, and soon there were hundreds of the animals throughout the islands. In time they became bothersome pests, eating the native vegetation and driving out other small animal life. Today wild goats still plague the islands and are shot on sight by Hawaiians.

Later, when cattle were first imported to the islands, many of these too were allowed to run wild. Their numbers greatly increased, and they have ruined many of the native forests by grazing on all available vegetation. Efforts to eliminate them have not been wholly successful.

THE FIRST HAWAIIAN KINGS
—AND A QUEEN

Early in the nineteenth century a Polynesian chief named Kamehameha united the people on the inhabited islands and established the Kingdom of Hawaii. The reign of Kamehameha I was followed by that of his son and then his grandson. Later, nephews and other close relatives continued the reign well into the latter part of the nineteenth century.

During this almost one-hundred-year period not only numerous Europeans but also many Americans visited the islands. When whaling became an important industry—whale oil was used as fuel for lamps before the days of electricity—the Hawaiian or Sandwich Islands were used as a supply station for American whaling ships from New England. In 1826 the United States negotiated an important early commercial trade treaty with Hawaii.

As interest in Hawaii began to grow, several European nations as well as the United States became more and more involved with Hawaii's government. Many of these foreigners were business people with major investments in the islands. There were also numerous religious missionaries from both Europe and the United States. To prevent being taken over by any of these

foreigners and the countries they represented, Hawaii declared its independence in 1844.

The Kamehameha male reign continued until 1891, when the male line died out and Queen Liliuokalani assumed the throne. The queen was determined to keep all foreign influence out of her government. But by this time there were a number of foreigners, including several Americans, who had lived on the islands for some time and wanted a say in the government. One of these Americans, Sanford B. Dole, led a bloodless revolution that established a republic headed by Dole. He was aided by eight other Americans, two Englishmen, and two Germans plus a number of American sailors and marines who were in ships just offshore. They landed, they said, to help keep the peace.

Dole wanted Hawaii to be annexed by the United States. This was finally done, and the territory of Hawaii was created in 1900 with Dole as the first governor. Hawaii was then governed as a U.S. territory for about sixty years. Gradually it began to assume an important place in the American economy as well as a strategic military role. Many requests were made for statehood by the Hawaiians, but all were refused.

THE IMPORTANCE OF PEARL HARBOR

Even before Hawaii became a territory, Pearl Harbor was turned over to the United States as a ship fuel and repair station. Soon

A statue of Kamehameha I, the Polynesian chief who united the island people and formed the Kingdom of Hawaii

afterward the United States began to build a huge naval base at Pearl Harbor. Barracks were built not only for American sailors but also for soldiers. One of the most famous of these was Schofield Barracks. Gradually Pearl Harbor became one of the key U.S. defense posts in the Pacific.

As World War II approached in the late 1930s, the U.S. government feared there might be a Japanese attack at any one of numerous American strongholds in the Pacific. But no one expected an attack on Pearl Harbor because it was so far away from the Japanese home islands. Even when the war in Europe began and United States military forces around the world were put on the alert, Pearl Harbor seemed an unlikely target. Nevertheless, the Japanese did open war on the United States with an aerial attack on Pearl Harbor on Sunday morning, December 7, 1941. This surprise attack was an enormous immediate success, from the Japanese viewpoint. Several American battleships were destroyed, and there were thousands of casualties.

Martial law was declared throughout Hawaii immediately after the Pearl Harbor attack, and civil government was not restored there until October of 1944 when the war was almost over. When the war did end, the people of Hawaii renewed their statehood requests. Their sons and daughters had fought well in the war, and they felt they deserved to be taken into the Union.

At first these renewed requests were again refused. But finally, on March 12, 1959, the United States Congress voted to admit Hawaii as the fiftieth state. President Dwight D. Eisenhower signed the official statehood proclamation on August 21, 1959.

FUTURE OF THE ALOHA STATE

In a normal year, tourism accounts for more than a third of the Aloha State's jobs and income. During the recent economic reces-

Beaches of the island paradise,
like Waikiki above, attract millions
of vacationers to Hawaii every year.

sion there were almost as many visitors as usual—4.2 million in 1982—but they spent far less. Hotel occupancy and revenues from the more expensive restaurants were down. Jewelry stores and souvenir shops also suffered from the lack of sales to visitors on tighter budgets.

Recently, too, Hawaiian sugar producers found themselves facing fierce competition from European Common Market countries whose sugar prices were being heavily subsidized by their governments. In addition, an international glut on the pineapple market occurred when foreign producers began saturating world markets with pineapple at reduced prices.

To replace lost revenue from these industries, an effort was being made in the early-1980s to develop Hawaii as a center for electronics and the production of mechanical robots (robotics) and computers. The state does not want heavy or "high smokestack" industry because of the damage it might do to the landscape and thus to the tourist industry.

The United States military is still a major pillar in the state's economy, and with increased military spending this pillar may become even more important. The annual payrolls for more than 60,000 U.S. servicemen and about 20,000 civilian employees, along with the money spent on the local purchase of supplies, amounts to almost two billion dollars.

Future battles loom over the possible rezoning of much of Hawaii's unused land for agriculture and other private business purposes. Almost half of the state's more than four million acres of land is owned by either the state or the federal government, and much of the rest is owned by several large corporations. In addition, land that is available for industrial development is very expensive. But, because most of Hawaii's food and goods are imported, the development of any local industries that will cut down the import bill will boost the Aloha State's economy.

The name Hawaii possibly comes from a Polynesian named Hawaii Loa who was thought to be the original discoverer of the islands. The name also may come from Hawaii or Hawaiki, the original home of the early Polynesians.

English, of course, is the official language and is spoken by most Hawaiians, but many ancestral Hawaiian words are used throughout the islands. Unlike the English alphabet the Hawaiian alphabet has only twelve letters, five vowels (a, e, i, o, and u) and the following seven consonants: h, k, l, m, n, p and w. Each vowel sound is pronounced separately, and the consonant w is sometimes pronounced like v. All Hawaiian words and syllables end with a vowel. Consonants are always separated by a vowel. Most words are accented on the next-to-last syllable. The first syllable of two-syllable words is accented.

year admitted to Union: 1959
capital: Honolulu
nickname: the Aloha State
motto: *Ua man ke ea o ka aina i ka pono*
    (The Life of the Land is Perpetuated
    in Righteousness)
flower: hibiscus
bird: nene or Hawaiian goose which is found only in Hawaii.
    It has long been threatened with extinction.
song: *Hawaii Ponoi* ("Our Own Hawaii")
flag: The eight main islands are represented by eight
    horizontal stripes, alternately red, white, and blue.

☆ ★ ☆

INDEX